er the sun
there is none.

till you find it;
ver mind it.

se

rd. On one hand,
you well if it motivates
, giving your worries
zing.

For every evil un‹
There is a remedy, o‹

If there be one, seek ‹
If there be none, n‹

Mother Go‹

Worrying is a double-edged sw‹
recognizing a problem will serve ‹
you to take action. On the othe‹
too much attention can be para‹

Break the habit of replaying negative outcomes in your mind by following these steps:

→ **WRITE.** Just putting a worry into words may be enough to defuse it.

→ **ACT.** If there is something you can do to change the situation, write down your plan and take action. If the source of your worry is completely out of your control, just acknowledging that can be a relief.

→ **TURN THE PAGE** and move on for a while. Choose a time in the future to check back, reflect, and record what happened and how you feel about it.

Remember that many worries do have a solution, and others never even come to pass. Keep track by tearing off the corner of an entry each time a worry disappears. ⟶

WORRY
CORNER

TODAY / /

This is my worry:

....

....

....

....

....

....

Can I do something about it?

Yes

....

Here is my plan:

→ ....

→ ....

→ ....

→ ....

→ ....

No

....

↓

Time to move on and check back later.

↑

CHECKING BACK AFTER
DAYS ...... WEEKS ...... MONTHS

What happened?

....
....
....
....
....
....

How I feel now:

....
....
....
....
....
....

No longer a worry? Tear off the tab. ⟶

WORRY CORNER

TODAY .../.../.....

This is my worry:

....
....
....
....
....
....

Can I do something about it?

Yes
....

Here is my plan:

→ ....
→ ....
→ ....
→ ....
→ ....

No
....

↓

Time to
move on
and check
back later.

↑

CHECKING BACK AFTER

DAYS ...... WEEKS ...... MONTHS

What happened?

....
....
....
....
....
....

How I feel now:

....
....
....
....
....
....

Don't fill your head
with worries.

There won't be room
for anything else.

LAOZI

No longer a worry? Tear off the tab. ⟶

WORRY
CORNER

This is my worry:

....

....

....

....

....

....

Can I do something about it?

Yes
....

Here is my plan:

→ ....

→ ....

→ ....

→ ....

→ ....

No
....

↓

Time to
move on
and check
back later.

↑

What happened?

....
....
....
....
....
....

How I feel now:

....
....
....
....
....
....

No longer a worry? Tear off the tab. ⟶

WORRY
CORNER

This is my worry:

....
....
....
....
....
....

Can I do something about it?

Yes
....

No
....

Here is my plan:

→ ....

→ ....

→ ....

→ ....

→ ....

Time to move on and check back later.

What happened?

....
....
....
....
....
....

How I feel now:

....
....
....
....
....
....

No longer a worry? Tear off the tab. ⟶

WORRY CORNER

A problem well stated is a problem half solved.

Charles Franklin Kettering

A TROUBLE SHARED IS A TROUBLE HALVED.

Dorothy L. Sayers

TODAY / /

This is my worry:

....
....
....
....
....
....

Can I do something about it?

Yes
....

Here is my plan:

→ ....

→ ....

→ ....

→ ....

→ ....

No
......

↓

Time to
move on
and check
back later.

↑

CHECKING BACK AFTER
DAYS ...... WEEKS ...... MONTHS

What happened?

....
....
....
....
....
....

How I feel now:

....
....
....
....
....
....

No longer a worry? Tear off the tab. ⟶

WORRY
CORNER

TODAY / /

This is my worry:

....

....

....

....

....

....

Can I do something about it?

Yes
....

Here is my plan:

→ ....

→ ....

→ ....

→ ....

→ ....

No
....

↓

Time to
move on
and check
back later.

↑

CHECKING BACK AFTER

DAYS   WEEKS   MONTHS
....

What happened?

....
....
....
....
....
....

How I feel now:

....
....
....
....
....
....

So always look for
the silver lining

And try to find
the sunny side of life.

P. G. WODEHOUSE

No longer a worry? Tear off the tab. ⟶

WORRY
CORNER

TODAY / /

This is my worry:

....
....
....
....
....
....

Can I do something about it?

Yes

Here is my plan:

→ ....
→ ....
→ ....
→ ....
→ ....

No

Time to move on and check back later.

CHECKING BACK AFTER
DAYS   WEEKS   MONTHS
....

What happened?

....
....
....
....
....
....

How I feel now:

....
....
....
....
....
....

No longer a worry? Tear off the tab. ⟶

WORRY
CORNER

TODAY / /

This is my worry:

....
....
....
....
....
....

Can I do something about it?

Yes
....

Here is my plan:

→ ....

→ ....

→ ....

→ ....

→ ....

No
....

↓

Time to move on and check back later.

↑

CHECKING BACK AFTER
...... DAYS ...... WEEKS ...... MONTHS

What happened?

....
....
....
....
....
....

How I feel now:

....
....
....
....
....
....

No longer a worry? Tear off the tab. ⟶

WORRY CORNER

WORRY IS RUST UPON THE BLADE.

Henry Ward Beecher

If your eyes are blinded
with your worries,
you cannot see
the beauty of the sunset.

J. Krishnamurti

TODAY / /
·················

This is my worry:

···
···
···
···
···
···

Can I do something about it?

Yes
···

Here is my plan:

→ ·································

→ ·································

→ ·································

→ ·································

→ ·································

No
········

↓

Time to move on and check back later.

↑

CHECKING BACK AFTER
DAYS   WEEKS   MONTHS
....

What happened?

....

....

....

....

....

....

How I feel now:

....

....

....

....

....

....

No longer a worry? Tear off the tab. ⟶

WORRY
CORNER

TODGY .... / .... / ....

This is my worry:

....
....
....
....
....
....

Can I do something about it?

Yes
....

Here is my plan:

→ ....

→ ....

→ ....

→ ....

→ ....

No
....

↓

Time to
move on
and check
back later.

↑

CHECKING BACK AFTER
...... DAYS ...... WEEKS ...... MONTHS

What happened?

....
....
....
....
....
....

How I feel now:

....
....
....
....
....
....

Don't hurry, don't worry.

You're only here for
a short visit.

So be sure to stop
and smell the flowers.

WALTER HAGEN

No longer a worry? Tear off the tab. ⟶

WORRY
CORNER

TODAY / /

This is my worry:

....
....
....
....
....
....

Can I do something about it?

Yes

....

Here is my plan:

→ ....

→ ....

→ ....

→ ....

→ ....

No

....

↓

Time to
move on
and check
back later.

↑

CHECKING BACK AFTER
DAYS · · · · · WEEKS · · · · · MONTHS

What happened?

....
....
....
....
....
....

How I feel now:

....
....
....
....
....
....

No longer a worry? Tear off the tab. ⟶

WORRY CORNER

TODY / /

This is my worry:

....
....
....
....
....
....

Can I do something about it?

Yes
....

Here is my plan:

→ ....

→ ....

→ ....

→ ....

→ ....

No
....

Time to
move on
and check
back later.

What happened?

....
....
....
....
....
....

How I feel now:

....
....
....
....
....
....

No longer a worry? Tear off the tab. ⟶

WORRY CORNER

EVERY CALAMITY IS A SPUR AND VALUABLE HINT.

Ralph Waldo Emerson

WHEN FORTUNE CLOSES ONE DOOR, IT OPENS ANOTHER.

Sa'di

TODY / /

This is my worry:

....
....
....
....
....
....

Can I do something about it?

Yes
....

Here is my plan:

→ ....

→ ....

→ ....

→ ....

→ ....

No
....

Time to
move on
and check
back later.

What happened?

· ·
· ·
· ·
· ·
· ·
· ·

How I feel now:

· ·
· ·
· ·
· ·
· ·
· ·

No longer a worry? Tear off the tab. ⟶

WORRY CORNER

TODAY / /

This is my worry:

....
....
....
....
....
....

Can I do something about it?

Yes
....

No
....

Here is my plan:

→ ....
→ ....
→ ....
→ ....
→ ....

↓

Time to
move on
and check
back later.

↑

What happened?

....
....
....
....
....
....

How I feel now:

....

....

....

....

....

....

Many a man curses the
rain that falls upon his
head, and knows not
that it brings abundance
to drive away hunger.

SAINT BASIL

No longer a worry? Tear off the tab. ⟶

WORRY
CORNER

TODY / /

This is my worry:

....
....
....
....
....
....

Can I do something about it?

Yes
....

Here is my plan:

→ ....

→ ....

→ ....

→ ....

→ ....

No
....

↓

Time to move on and check back later.

↑

CHECKING BACK AFTER
DAYS   WEEKS   MONTHS
....

What happened?

....
....
....
....
....
....

How I feel now:

....
....
....
....
....
....

No longer a worry? Tear off the tab. ⟶

WORRY CORNER

This is my worry:

....
....
....
....
....
....

Can I do something about it?

Yes ....

Here is my plan:

→ ....
→ ....
→ ....
→ ....
→ ....

No ....

↓

Time to
move on
and check
back later.

↑

What happened?

....
....
....
....
....
....

How I feel now:

....
....
....
....
....
....

No longer a worry? Tear off the tab. ⟶

WORRY
CORNER

ACTION IS WORRY'S WORST ENEMY.

American proverb

Problems are only opportunities in work clothes.

Henry J. Kaiser

TODODAY / /

This is my worry:

....
....
....
....
....
....

Can I do something about it?

Yes
....

Here is my plan:

→ ....

→ ....

→ ....

→ ....

→ ....

No
....

↓

Time to move on and check back later.

What happened?

....
....
....
....
....
....

How I feel now:

....
....
....
....
....
....

No longer a worry? Tear off the tab. ⟶

WORRY
CORNER

This is my worry:

....
....
....
....
....
....

Can I do something about it?

Yes

....

Here is my plan:

→ ....

→ ....

→ ....

→ ....

→ ....

No

....

↓

Time to move on and check back later.

What happened?

⋯⋯⋯⋯⋯⋯⋯⋯⋯⋯⋯⋯⋯⋯⋯⋯⋯⋯⋯⋯⋯⋯⋯⋯⋯⋯⋯⋯

⋯⋯⋯⋯⋯⋯⋯⋯⋯⋯⋯⋯⋯⋯⋯⋯⋯⋯⋯⋯⋯⋯⋯⋯⋯⋯⋯⋯

⋯⋯⋯⋯⋯⋯⋯⋯⋯⋯⋯⋯⋯⋯⋯⋯⋯⋯⋯⋯⋯⋯⋯⋯⋯⋯⋯⋯

⋯⋯⋯⋯⋯⋯⋯⋯⋯⋯⋯⋯⋯⋯⋯⋯⋯⋯⋯⋯⋯⋯⋯⋯⋯⋯⋯⋯

⋯⋯⋯⋯⋯⋯⋯⋯⋯⋯⋯⋯⋯⋯⋯⋯⋯⋯⋯⋯⋯⋯⋯⋯⋯⋯⋯⋯

⋯⋯⋯⋯⋯⋯⋯⋯⋯⋯⋯⋯⋯⋯⋯⋯⋯⋯⋯⋯⋯⋯⋯⋯⋯⋯⋯⋯

How I feel now:

⋯⋯⋯⋯⋯⋯⋯⋯⋯⋯⋯⋯⋯⋯

⋯⋯⋯⋯⋯⋯⋯⋯⋯⋯⋯⋯⋯⋯

⋯⋯⋯⋯⋯⋯⋯⋯⋯⋯⋯⋯⋯⋯

⋯⋯⋯⋯⋯⋯⋯⋯⋯⋯⋯⋯⋯⋯   **Troubles are like babies—
they only grow by nursing.**

⋯⋯⋯⋯⋯⋯⋯⋯⋯⋯⋯⋯⋯⋯   DOUGLAS WILLIAM JERROLD

⋯⋯⋯⋯⋯⋯⋯⋯⋯⋯⋯⋯⋯⋯

No longer a worry? Tear off the tab. ⟶

WORRY
CORNER

TODAY / /

This is my worry:

....
....
....
....
....
....

Can I do something about it?

Yes

Here is my plan:

→ ....
→ ....
→ ....
→ ....
→ ....

No

↓

Time to move on and check back later.

↑

What happened?

....
....
....
....
....
....

How I feel now:

....
....
....
....
....
....

No longer a worry? Tear off the tab. ⟶

WORRY CORNER

TODAY / /

This is my worry:

....

....

....

....

....

....

Can I do something about it?

Yes

....

Here is my plan:

→ ....

→ ....

→ ....

→ ....

→ ....

No

....

↓

Time to move on and check back later.

CHECKING BACK AFTER
DAYS   WEEKS   MONTHS
······   ······   ······

What happened?

....
....
....
....
....
....

How I feel now:

....
....
....
....
....
....

No longer a worry? Tear off the tab. ⟶

WORRY
CORNER

There are no impossible obstacles; there are just stronger and weaker wills, that's all!

Jules Verne

A day of worry
is more exhausting
than a week of work.

John Lubbock

This is my worry:

....
....
....
....
....
....

Can I do something about it?

Yes

....

Here is my plan:

→ ....

→ ....

→ ....

→ ....

→ ....

No

↓

Time to
move on
and check
back later.

↑

What happened?

....
....
....
....
....
....

How I feel now:

....
....
....
....
....
....

No longer a worry? Tear off the tab. ⟶

WORRY
CORNER

TODAY / /
....

This is my worry:

....
....
....
....
....
....

Can I do something about it?

Yes
....

Here is my plan:

→ ....

→ ....

→ ....

→ ....

→ ....

No
....

↓

Time to
move on
and check
back later.

↑

What happened?

....
....
....
....
....
....

How I feel now:

....
....
....
....
....
....

> You'll break the worry habit the day you decide you can meet and master the worst that can happen to you.
>
> ARNOLD H. GLASOW

No longer a worry? Tear off the tab. ⟶

WORRY CORNER

TODAY / /

This is my worry:

....

....

....

....

....

....

Can I do something about it?

Yes   **No**
....

Here is my plan: ↓

→ ....   **Time to**
                                                                move on
→ ....   **and check**
                                                               back later.
→ ....

→ ....   ↑

→ ....

CHECKING BACK AFTER
...... DAYS ...... WEEKS ...... MONTHS

What happened?

....

....

....

....

....

....

How I feel now:

....

....

....

....

....

....

No longer a worry? Tear off the tab. ⟶

WORRY
CORNER

TODAY ..... / ..... / .....

This is my worry:

....
....
....
....
....
....

Can I do something about it?

Yes
....

Here is my plan:

→ ....

→ ....

→ ....

→ ....

→ ....

No
.....

Time to move on and check back later.

What happened?

....
....
....
....
....
....

How I feel now:

....
....
....
....
....
....

No longer a worry? Tear off the tab. ⟶

WORRY CORNER

It only seems as if
you are doing something
when you're worrying.

Lucy Maud Montgomery

Worrying is like a rocking chair;
it gives you something to do,
but it gets you nowhere.

Glenn Turner

TODAY / /

This is my worry:

....
....
....
....
....
....

Can I do something about it?

Yes
....

Here is my plan:

→ ....

→ ....

→ ....

→ ....

→ ....

No
....

↓

Time to move on and check back later.

↑
_____

CHECKING BACK AFTER
DAYS · · · · · · WEEKS · · · · · · MONTHS

What happened?

· ·

· ·

· ·

· ·

· ·

How I feel now:

· ·

· ·

· ·

· ·

· ·

No longer a worry? Tear off the tab. ⟶

WORRY CORNER

TODAY / /

This is my worry:

....
....
....
....
....
....

Can I do something about it?

Yes

No

Here is my plan:

→ ....

→ ....

→ ....

→ ....

→ ....

Time to move on and check back later.

What happened?

....

....

....

....

....

....

How I feel now:

....

....

....

....

....

....

It helps to write down half a dozen things which are worrying me. Two of them, say, disappear; about two nothing can be done, so it's no use worrying; and two perhaps can be settled.

WINSTON CHURCHILL

No longer a worry? Tear off the tab. ⟶

WORRY CORNER

TODAY / /

This is my worry:

....

....

....

....

....

....

Can I do something about it?

Yes
....

No
......

Here is my plan:

→ ....

→ ....

→ ....

→ ....

→ ....

Time to
move on
and check
back later.

CHECKING BACK AFTER

DAYS   WEEKS   MONTHS

....

What happened?

....
....
....
....
....
....

How I feel now:

....
....
....
....
....
....

No longer a worry? Tear off the tab. ⟶

WORRY CORNER

TODAY / /

This is my worry:

....
....
....
....
....
....

Can I do something about it?

Yes

Here is my plan:

→ ....
→ ....
→ ....
→ ....
→ ....

No

↓

Time to move on and check back later.

↑

CHECKING BACK AFTER

DAYS · · · · · · WEEKS · · · · · · MONTHS

What happened?

....
....
....
....
....
....

How I feel now:

....
....
....
....
....
....

No longer a worry? Tear off the tab. ⟶

WORRY CORNER

Drag your thoughts away from your troubles—by the ears, by the heels, or any other way, so you manage it.

Mark Twain

You can't wring your hands
and roll up your sleeves
at the same time.

Pat Schroeder

TODAY / /

This is my worry:

....

....

....

....

....

....

Can I do something about it?

Yes

....

Here is my plan:

→ ....

→ ....

→ ....

→ ....

→ ....

No

....

↓

Time to move on and check back later.

↑

What happened?

....
....
....
....
....
....

How I feel now:

....
....
....
....
....
....

No longer a worry? Tear off the tab. ⟶

WORRY CORNER

TODAY ...... / ...... / ......

This is my worry:

....

....

....

....

....

....

Can I do something about it?

Yes
....

Here is my plan:

→ ....

→ ....

→ ....

→ ....

→ ....

No
......

↓

Time to move on and check back later.

CHECKING BACK AFTER
DAYS   WEEKS   MONTHS
....

What happened?

....
....
....
....
....
....

How I feel now:

....
....
....
....
....
....

There is no good in arguing
with the inevitable. The
only argument available
with an east wind is to put
on your overcoat.

JAMES RUSSELL LOWELL

No longer a worry? Tear off the tab. ⟶

WORRY
CORNER

TODAY ...../...../.....

This is my worry:

....
....
....
....
....
....

Can I do something about it?

Yes
....

Here is my plan:

→ ....
→ ....
→ ....
→ ....
→ ....

No
....

↓

Time to move on and check back later.

↑

CHECKING BACK AFTER
DAYS · · · · · · WEEKS · · · · · · MONTHS

What happened?

· ·

How I feel now:

· ·

No longer a worry? Tear off the tab. ⟶

WORRY CORNER

TODAY / /

This is my worry:

....
....
....
....
....
....

Can I do something about it?

Yes
....

Here is my plan:

→ ....

→ ....

→ ....

→ ....

→ ....

No
....

↓

Time to
move on
and check
back later.

↑

CHECKING BACK AFTER
DAYS ...... WEEKS ...... MONTHS

What happened?

....
....
....
....
....
....

How I feel now:

....
....
....
....
....
....

No longer a worry? Tear off the tab. ⟶

WORRY CORNER

A hundredload of worry will not pay an ounce of debt.

George Herbert

Worry is interest paid on trouble before it falls due.

William Ralph Inge

TODAY ___/___/___

This is my worry:

....
....
....
....
....
....

Can I do something about it?

Yes
....

Here is my plan:

→ ....
→ ....
→ ....
→ ....
→ ....

No
....

↓

Time to move on and check back later.

↑

CHECKING BACK AFTER
DAYS ...... WEEKS ...... MONTHS

What happened?

....
....
....
....
....
....

How I feel now:

....
....
....
....
....
....

No longer a worry? Tear off the tab. ⟶

WORRY CORNER

This is my worry:

....
....
....
....
....
....

Can I do something about it?

Yes
....

Here is my plan:

→ ....
→ ....
→ ....
→ ....
→ ....

No
....

↓

Time to
move on
and check
back later.

CHECKING BACK AFTER

DAYS ...... WEEKS ...... MONTHS ......

What happened?

....
....
....
....
....
....

How I feel now:

....
....
....
....
....
....

Do not anticipate trouble, or worry about what may never happen. Keep in the sunlight.

BENJAMIN FRANKLIN

No longer a worry? Tear off the tab. ⟶

WORRY CORNER

This is my worry:

....
....
....
....
....
....

Can I do something about it?

Yes
....

Here is my plan:

→ ....
→ ....
→ ....
→ ....
→ ....

No
↓

Time to move on and check back later.

CHECKING BACK AFTER

DAYS   WEEKS   MONTHS

What happened?

....

....

....

....

....

....

How I feel now:

....

....

....

....

....

....

No longer a worry? Tear off the tab. ———→

This is my worry:

....
....
....
....
....
....

Can I do something about it?

Yes
....

Here is my plan:

→ ....

→ ....

→ ....

→ ....

→ ....

No
....

↓

Time to
move on
and check
back later.

↑

CHECKING BACK AFTER
DAYS ...... WEEKS ...... MONTHS

What happened?

....
....
....
....
....
....

How I feel now:

....
....
....
....
....
....

No longer a worry? Tear off the tab. ⟶

WORRY CORNER

He suffers more than necessary, who suffers before it is necessary.

Lucius Annaeus Seneca

DON'T MEET
TROUBLES HALFWAY.

Michael Sadleir

TODAY / /
....

This is my worry:

....
....
....
....
....
....

Can I do something about it?

Yes
....

Here is my plan:

→ ....
→ ....
→ ....
→ ....
→ ....

No
....

↓

Time to move on and check back later.

↑

CHECKING BACK AFTER

DAYS WEEKS MONTHS
....

What happened?

....

....

....

....

....

....

How I feel now:

....

....

....

....

....

....

No longer a worry? Tear off the tab. ⟶

WORRY CORNER

TODAY / /

This is my worry:

....
....
....
....
....
....

Can I do something about it?

Yes
....

Here is my plan:

→ ....
→ ....
→ ....
→ ....
→ ....

No
......

Time to move on and check back later.

What happened?

....
....
....
....
....
....

How I feel now:

....
....
....
....
....
....

Worry pulls
tomorrow's cloud
over today's sunshine.

CHARLES R. SWINDOLL

No longer a worry? Tear off the tab. ⟶

WORRY
CORNER

TODAY   /   /

This is my worry:

....
....
....
....
....
....

Can I do something about it?

Yes
....

Here is my plan:

→ ....

→ ....

→ ....

→ ....

→ ....

No
....

↓

Time to move on and check back later.

↑

What happened?

....
....
....
....
....
....

How I feel now:

....
....
....
....
....
....

No longer a worry? Tear off the tab. ⟶

WORRY
CORNER

TODAY / /

This is my worry:

....
....
....
....
....
....

Can I do something about it?

Yes
....

Here is my plan:

→ ....

→ ....

→ ....

→ ....

→ ....

No
.....

↓

Time to move on and check back later.

↑

What happened?

....
....
....
....
....
....

How I feel now:

....
....
....
....
....
....

No longer a worry? Tear off the tab. ⟶

WORRY CORNER

It is the little
things that fret
and worry us;
you can dodge
an elephant,
but not a fly.

Josh Billings

Worry often gives a small thing a big shadow.

Swedish proverb

TODAY / /

This is my worry:

....

....

....

....

....

....

Can I do something about it?

Yes
....

Here is my plan:

→ ....

→ ....

→ ....

→ ....

→ ....

No
....

Time to
move on
and check
back later.

CHECKING BACK AFTER

DAYS   WEEKS   MONTHS

....

What happened?

....

....

....

....

....

....

How I feel now:

....

....

....

....

....

....

No longer a worry? Tear off the tab. ⟶

WORRY CORNER

TODY / /

This is my worry:

....
....
....
....
....
....

Can I do something about it?

Yes   **No**
....

Here is my plan: ↓

→ ....   Time to
move on
→ ....   and check
back later.
→ ....

→ ....

→ ....   ↰

What happened?

....
....
....
....
....
....

How I feel now:

....
....
....
....
....
....

If you see ten troubles coming down the road, you can be sure that nine will run into the ditch before they reach you.

CALVIN COOLIDGE

No longer a worry? Tear off the tab. ⟶

WORRY CORNER

TODAY ___/___/___

This is my worry:

....
....
....
....
....
....

Can I do something about it?

Yes   **No**
....

Here is my plan: |
                                                                 ↓
→ ....   **Time to**
                                                             move on
→ ....   **and check**
                                                             back later.
→ ....

→ ....   ↑

→ ....   _____|

What happened?

....

....

....

....

....

....

How I feel now:

....

....

....

....

....

....

No longer a worry? Tear off the tab. ⟶

WORRY CORNER

TODAY / /

This is my worry:

....
....
....
....
....
....

Can I do something about it?

Yes

Here is my plan:

→ ....
→ ....
→ ....
→ ....
→ ....

No

Time to move on and check back later.

What happened?

· ·

· ·

· ·

· ·

· ·

· ·

How I feel now:

· ·

· ·

· ·

· ·

· ·

· ·

No longer a worry? Tear off the tab. ⟶

WORRY CORNER

Rule No. 1 is, don't sweat the small stuff.

Robert Eliot

Rule No. 2 is, it's all small stuff.

Robert Eliot

TODAY ../ . /..

This is my worry:

....
....
....
....
....
....

Can I do something about it?

Yes
....

Here is my plan:

→ ....

→ ....

→ ....

→ ....

→ ....

No
......

Time to move on and check back later.

CHECKING BACK AFTER

DAYS ⋯⋯ WEEKS ⋯⋯ MONTHS

What happened?

....
....
....
....
....
....

How I feel now:

....
....
....
....
....
....

No longer a worry? Tear off the tab. ⟶

WORRY
CORNER

TODAY ..... / ..... / .....

This is my worry:

....
....
....
....
....
....

Can I do something about it?

Yes
....

Here is my plan:

→ ....

→ ....

→ ....

→ ....

→ ....

No
.....

Time to move on and check back later.

CHECKING BACK AFTER

DAYS ...... WEEKS ...... MONTHS

What happened?

....
....
....
....
....
....

How I feel now:

....
....
....
....
....
....

Don't be concerned about whether people are watching you or criticizing you. The chances are that they aren't paying any attention to you.

ELEANOR ROOSEVELT

No longer a worry? Tear off the tab. ⟶

WORRY CORNER

TODAY / /

This is my worry:

....
....
....
....
....
....

Can I do something about it?

Yes
....

Here is my plan:

→ ....

→ ....

→ ....

→ ....

→ ....

No
....

↓

Time to move on and check back later.

↑

What happened?

....

....

....

....

....

....

How I feel now:

....

....

....

....

....

....

No longer a worry? Tear off the tab. ⟶

WORRY
CORNER

This is my worry:

....
....
....
....
....
....

Can I do something about it?

Yes
....

Here is my plan:

→ ....

→ ....

→ ....

→ ....

→ ....

No
....

↓

Time to move on and check back later.

↑

What happened?

··
··
··
··
··
··

How I feel now:

··
··
··
··
··
··

No longer a worry? Tear off the tab. ⟶

WORRY
CORNER

My life has been full
of terrible misfortunes,
most of which
never happened.

Michel de Montaigne

LOOK BACK, AND SMILE ON PERILS PAST!

Sir Walter Scott

This is my worry:

....
....
....
....
....
....

Can I do something about it?

Yes
....

Here is my plan:

→ ....
→ ....
→ ....
→ ....
→ ....

No
....

↓

Time to move on and check back later.

What happened?

....
....
....
....
....
....

How I feel now:

....
....
....
....
....
....

No longer a worry? Tear off the tab. ⟶

WORRY CORNER

TODY / /

This is my worry:

....
....
....
....
....
....

Can I do something about it?

Yes
....

Here is my plan:

→ ....

→ ....

→ ....

→ ....

→ ....

No
....

↓

Time to
move on
and check
back later.

↑

What happened?

....
....
....
....
....
....

How I feel now:

....
....
....
....
....
....

Each minute we spend worrying about the future and regretting the past is a minute we miss in our appointment with life.

THICH NHAT HANH

No longer a worry? Tear off the tab. ⟶

WORRY CORNER

TODAY   /   /

This is my worry:

....
....
....
....
....
....

Can I do something about it?

Yes
....

Here is my plan:

→   ....

→   ....

→   ....

→   ....

→   ....

No
......

↓

Time to
move on
and check
back later.

↑

CHECKING BACK AFTER
DAYS WEEKS MONTHS

What happened?

....
....
....
....
....
....

How I feel now:

....
....
....
....
....
....

No longer a worry? Tear off the tab. ⟶

WORRY
CORNER

TODAY / /
···········

This is my worry:

···
···
···
···
···
···

Can I do something about it?

Yes
···

No
·········

Here is my plan:

→ ···

→ ···

→ ···

→ ···

→ ···

Time to
move on
and check
back later.

CHECKING BACK AFTER
...... DAYS ...... WEEKS ...... MONTHS

What happened?

....
....
....
....
....
....

How I feel now:

....
....
....
....
....
....

No longer a worry? Tear off the tab. ⟶

WORRY CORNER

Even in the deepest sinking there is the hidden purpose of an ultimate rising.

Hasidic saying

LOOK NOT THOU DOWN BUT UP!

Robert Browning

TODAY / /

This is my worry:

....
....
....
....
....
....

Can I do something about it?

Yes

Here is my plan:

→ ....
→ ....
→ ....
→ ....
→ ....

No

↓

Time to move on and check back later.

↑

CHECKING BACK AFTER
DAYS   WEEKS   MONTHS
....

What happened?

....

....

....

....

....

....

How I feel now:

....

....

....

....

....

....

No longer a worry? Tear off the tab. ⟶

WORRY CORNER

This is my worry:

....
....
....
....
....
....

Can I do something about it?

Yes

No

....

Here is my plan:

→ ....

→ ....

→ ....

→ ....

→ ....

Time to
move on
and check
back later.

CHECKING BACK AFTER
DAYS · · · · · WEEKS · · · · · MONTHS

What happened?

....
....
....
....
....
....

How I feel now:

....
....
....
....
....
....

> If we had no winter, the spring would not be so pleasant; if we did not sometimes taste of adversity, prosperity would not be so welcome.
>
> **ANNE BRADSTREET**

No longer a worry? Tear off the tab. ⟶

WORRY CORNER

TODAY / /

This is my worry:

....
....
....
....
....
....

Can I do something about it?

Yes

No

Here is my plan:

→ ....

→ ....

→ ....

→ ....

→ ....

Time to move on and check back later.

What happened?

....
....
....
....
....
....

How I feel now:

....
....
....
....
....
....

No longer a worry? Tear off the tab. ⟶

WORRY CORNER

TODAY / /

This is my worry:

....
....
....
....
....
....

Can I do something about it?

Yes   **No**

Here is my plan:

→ ....

→ ....

→ ....

→ ....

→ ....

Time to move on and check back later.

What happened?

....
....
....
....
....
....

How I feel now:

....
....
....
....
....
....

No longer a worry? Tear off the tab. ⟶

WORRY
CORNER

I highly
recommend
worrying.
It is much
more effective
than dieting.

William Powell

SWEET ARE THE USES OF ADVERSITY.

William Shakespeare

This is my worry:

....
....
....
....
....
....

Can I do something about it?

Yes

....

Here is my plan:

→ ....

→ ....

→ ....

→ ....

→ ....

No

↓

Time to
move on
and check
back later.

↑

What happened?

....

....

....

....

....

....

How I feel now:

....

....

....

....

....

....

No longer a worry? Tear off the tab. ⟶

WORRY CORNER

TODY / /

This is my worry:

....
....
....
....
....
....

Can I do something about it?

Yes   **No**
....

Here is my plan: |
                                                                ↓
→ ....   **Time to**
                                                      move on
→ ....   **and check**
                                                      back later.
→ ....

→ ....

→ .... ⌐→

CHECKING BACK AFTER

DAYS · · · · · · WEEKS · · · · · · MONTHS

What happened?

· ·
· ·
· ·
· ·
· ·
· ·

How I feel now:

· ·
· ·
· ·
·   **Worries go down better**
·   **with soup.**
· ·
                                                                 JEWISH PROVERB

No longer a worry? Tear off the tab. ⟶

WORRY CORNER

TODAY ..../..../....

This is my worry:

....
....
....
....
....
....

Can I do something about it?

Yes
....

Here is my plan:

→ ....

→ ....

→ ....

→ ....

→ ....

No
....

↓

Time to
move on
and check
back later.

↑

What happened?

....
....
....
....
....
....

How I feel now:

....
....
....
....
....
....

No longer a worry? Tear off the tab. ⟶

WORRY
CORNER

This is my worry:

....
....
....
....
....
....

Can I do something about it?

Yes
....

Here is my plan:

→ ....
→ ....
→ ....
→ ....
→ ....

No
....

↓

Time to move on and check back later.

↑

CHECKING BACK AFTER
DAYS   WEEKS   MONTHS

What happened?

....

....

....

....

....

....

How I feel now:

....

....

....

....

....

....

No longer a worry? Tear off the tab. ⟶

WORRY CORNER

WHEN IT RAINS, LOOK FOR RAINBOWS.

Anonymous

WHEN IT IS DARK, LOOK FOR STARS.

Anonymous

TODY / /

This is my worry:

....

....

....

....

....

....

Can I do something about it?

Yes

....

Here is my plan:

→ ....

→ ....

→ ....

→ ....

→ ....

No

.....

Time to
move on
and check
back later.

CHECKING BACK AFTER
DAYS   WEEKS   MONTHS
....

What happened?

....
....
....
....
....
....

How I feel now:

....
....
....
....
....
....

No longer a worry? Tear off the tab. ⟶

WORRY CORNER

This is my worry:

....
....
....
....
....
....

Can I do something about it?

Yes
......

Here is my plan:

→ ....
→ ....
→ ....
→ ....
→ ....

No
....

↓

Time to move on and check back later.

↑

What happened?

....
....
....
....
....
....

How I feel now:

....
....
....
....
....
....

The best way to cheer yourself is to try to cheer somebody else up.

MARK TWAIN

No longer a worry? Tear off the tab. ⟶

WORRY CORNER

TODAY / /

This is my worry:

....

....

....

....

....

....

Can I do something about it?

Yes

No

Here is my plan:

→ ....

→ ....

→ ....

→ ....

→ ....

Time to move on and check back later.

CHECKING BACK AFTER
DAYS   WEEKS   MONTHS
....

What happened?

....
....
....
....
....
....

How I feel now:

....
....
....
....
....
....

No longer a worry? Tear off the tab. ⟶

WORRY
CORNER

TODAY / /

This is my worry:

....
....
....
....
....
....

Can I do something about it?

Yes

Here is my plan:

→ ....
→ ....
→ ....
→ ....
→ ....

No

↓

Time to
move on
and check
back later.

↑

What happened?

....
....
....
....
....
....

How I feel now:

....
....
....
....
....
....

No longer a worry? Tear off the tab. ⟶

WORRY CORNER

There are times when
we cannot see
one step ahead of us,
but five years later
we are eating and
sleeping somewhere.

Chrysis

SOMETHING WILL TURN UP.

Charles Dickens

TODAY .../ .../ ...

This is my worry:

....
....
....
....
....
....

Can I do something about it?

Yes

....

Here is my plan:

→ ....

→ ....

→ ....

→ ....

→ ....

No

....

↓

Time to move on and check back later.

↑

CHECKING BACK AFTER
DAYS   WEEKS   MONTHS
······   ······   ······

What happened?

....
....
....
....
....
....

How I feel now:

....
....
....
....
....
....

No longer a worry? Tear off the tab. ⟶

WORRY CORNER

TODAY .../.../.....

This is my worry:

....
....
....
....
....
....

Can I do something about it?

Yes
....

Here is my plan:

→ ....

→ ....

→ ....

→ ....

→ ....

No
......

↓

Time to
move on
and check
back later.

↑

CHECKING BACK AFTER
DAYS   WEEKS   MONTHS

What happened?

....
....
....
....
....
....

How I feel now:

....
....
....
....
....
....

The worse the Passage,
the more welcome the Port.

THOMAS FULLER

No longer a worry? Tear off the tab. ——➤

WORRY CORNER

TODAY / /

This is my worry:

....
....
....
....
....
....

Can I do something about it?

Yes
....

Here is my plan:

→ ....

→ ....

→ ....

→ ....

→ ....

No

↓

Time to
move on
and check
back later.

↑

CHECKING BACK AFTER
DAYS ...... WEEKS ...... MONTHS

What happened?

....
....
....
....
....
....

How I feel now:

....
....
....
....
....
....

No longer a worry? Tear off the tab. ⟶

WORRY CORNER

TODY / /

This is my worry:

....
....
....
....
....
....

Can I do something about it?

Yes
....

Here is my plan:

→ ....

→ ....

→ ....

→ ....

→ ....

No

↓

Time to move on and check back later.

↑

CHECKING BACK AFTER
DAYS   WEEKS   MONTHS

What happened?

....
....
....
....
....
....

How I feel now:

....
....
....
....
....
....

No longer a worry? Tear off the tab. ——→

WORRY CORNER

What's the use of worrying?
It never was worth while, so
Pack up your troubles
in your old kit-bag
And smile, smile, smile.

World War I marching song

BE A WARRIOR, NOT A WORRIER.

Anonymous

This is my worry:

....

....

....

....

....

....

Can I do something about it?

Yes

....

Here is my plan:

→ ....

→ ....

→ ....

→ ....

→ ....

No

....

↓

**Time to
move on
and check
back later.**

↑

CHECKING BACK AFTER
DAYS · · · · · · WEEKS · · · · · · MONTHS

What happened?

. . . .
. . . .
. . . .
. . . .
. . . .
. . . .

How I feel now:

. . . .
. . . .
. . . .
. . . .
. . . .
. . . .

No longer a worry? Tear off the tab. ⎯⎯⎯→

WORRY CORNER

TODAY   /   /   ....

This is my worry:

....
....
....
....
....
....

Can I do something about it?

Yes   **No**
....

Here is my plan: ↓

→ ....

→ ....   **Time to**
                                                            move on
→ ....   **and check**
                                                            back later.
→ ....

→ ....   ↑

CHECKING BACK AFTER
DAYS · · · · · WEEKS · · · · · MONTHS

What happened?

· ·

· ·

· ·

· ·

· ·

· ·

How I feel now:

There are two days in the week about which and upon which I never worry. . . . One of these days is Yesterday. . . . And the other day I do not worry about is Tomorrow.

ROBERT J. BURDETTE

No longer a worry? Tear off the tab. ⟶

WORRY CORNER

This is my worry:

....
....
....
....
....
....

Can I do something about it?

Yes
....

Here is my plan:

→ ....

→ ....

→ ....

→ ....

→ ....

No
....

↓

Time to move on and check back later.

↑

What happened?

....
....
....
....
....
....

How I feel now:

....
....
....
....
....

No longer a worry? Tear off the tab. ⟶

WORRY CORNER

This is my worry:

....
....
....
....
....
....

Can I do something about it?

Yes

No

Here is my plan:

→ ....

→ ....

→ ....

→ ....

→ ....

Time to move on and check back later.

What happened?

....
....
....
....
....
....

How I feel now:

....
....
....
....
....
....

No longer a worry? Tear off the tab. ⟶

WORRY CORNER

You cannot prevent
the birds of sorrow from
flying over your head,
but you can prevent them
from building nests
in your hair.

Chinese proverb

Hope is the thing
with feathers
That perches in the soul,
And sings the tune
without the words,
And never stops at all.

Emily Dickinson

TODAY / /

This is my worry:

....
....
....
....
....
....

Can I do something about it?

Yes
....

Here is my plan:

→ ....
→ ....
→ ....
→ ....
→ ....

No
......

Time to move on and check back later.

CHECKING BACK AFTER
DAYS ...... WEEKS ...... MONTHS

What happened?

....
....
....
....
....
....

How I feel now:

....
....
....
....
....
....

No longer a worry? Tear off the tab. ⟶

WORRY
CORNER

TODAY / /

This is my worry:

....

....

....

....

....

....

Can I do something about it?

Yes

....

Here is my plan:

→ ....

→ ....

→ ....

→ ....

→ ....

No

↓

Time to move on and check back later.

CHECKING BACK AFTER
DAYS ...... WEEKS ...... MONTHS ......

What happened?

....
....
....
....
....
....

How I feel now:

....
....
....
....
....
....

Nothing contributes so much to tranquilize the mind as a steady purpose.

MARY SHELLEY

No longer a worry? Tear off the tab. ⟶

WORRY CORNER

TODAY / /

This is my worry:

....
....
....
....
....
....

Can I do something about it?

Yes
....

Here is my plan:

→ ....
→ ....
→ ....
→ ....
→ ....

No

↓

Time to
move on
and check
back later.

↑

CHECKING BACK AFTER

DAYS   WEEKS   MONTHS
....

What happened?

....

....

....

....

....

....

How I feel now:

....

....

....

....

....

....

No longer a worry? Tear off the tab. ⟶

WORRY CORNER

TODAY / /

This is my worry:

....
....
....
....
....
....

Can I do something about it?

Yes | **No**
.... | ......

Here is my plan:

→ ....

→ ....

→ ....

→ ....

→ ....

Time to move on and check back later.

What happened?

....
....
....
....
....
....

How I feel now:

....

....

....

....

....

....

> I am reminded of the
> advice of my neighbor.
> "Never worry about your
> heart till it stops beating."
>
> E. B. WHITE

No longer a worry? Tear off the tab. ——⟶

WORRY
CORNER

Concept and text by Dian G. Smith and Robie Rogge

Designer: Hana Anouk Nakamura

ISBN: 978-1-4197-1919-6

Copyright © 2016 ROBIE LLC

Printed and bound in China
10 9 8 7 6 5 4 3

Abrams Noterie products are available at special discounts when purchased in quantity
for premiums and promotions as well as fundraising or educational use. Special editions
can also be created to specification. For details, contact specialsales@abramsbooks.com
or the address below.

ABRAMS The Art of Books
115 West 18th Street, New York, NY 10011
abramsbooks.com